DALAI LAMA QUOTES

DALAI LAMA

Copyright © Dalai Lama
All Rights Reserved.

This book has been self-published with all reasonable efforts taken to make the material error-free by the author. No part of this book shall be used, reproduced in any manner whatsoever without written permission from the author, except in the case of brief quotations embodied in critical articles and reviews.

The Author of this book is solely responsible and liable for its content including but not limited to the views, representations, descriptions, statements, information, opinions and references ["Content"]. The Content of this book shall not constitute or be construed or deemed to reflect the opinion or expression of the Publisher or Editor. Neither the Publisher nor Editor endorse or approve the Content of this book or guarantee the reliability, accuracy or completeness of the Content published herein and do not make any representations or warranties of any kind, express or implied, including but not limited to the implied warranties of merchantability, fitness for a particular purpose. The Publisher and Editor shall not be liable whatsoever for any errors, omissions, whether such errors or omissions result from negligence, accident, or any other cause or claims for loss or damages of any kind, including without limitation, indirect or consequential loss or damage arising out of use, inability to use, or about the reliability, accuracy or sufficiency of the information contained in this book.

Made with ♥ on the Notion Press Platform
www.notionpress.com

This book is the collection of all the quotes by dalali lama . He is most recognizable figure in Tibetan Buddhism. He is renowned for his promotion of peace and compassion. His teachings have brought him fame and reverence from Buddhists and non-Buddhists alike.

Contents

Foreword   *vii*

Part 1

Part 2

Part 3

Part 4

Part 5

Part 6

Part 7

Part 8

Part 9

Part 10

Part 11

Part 12

Part 13

Part 14

Part 15

Part 16

Part 17

Part 18

Part 19

Part 20

Part 21

Part 22

Part 23

Part 24

Part 25

Part 26

Part 27

Contents

Part 28

Part 29

Part 30

Part 31

Part 32

Part 33

Part 34

Part 35

Part 36

Part 37

Part 38

Part 39

Part 40

Part 41

Part 42

Part 43

Part 44

Part 45

Part 46

Part 47

Part 48

Part 49

Part 50

Foreword

Dalai lama is a inspiration for me and for every youth. After reading their books (Art of happiness and other). I decided to compiled them in the book which is really going to help you.

"If a problem can be solved it will be. If it can not be solved there is no use worrying about it."

"Our visit to this planet is short, so we should use our time meaningfully, which we can do by helping others wherever possible."

"To be aware of a single shortcoming in oneself is more useful than to be aware of a thousand in someone else."

"Sometimes one creates a dynamic impression by saying something, and sometimes one creates as significant an impression by remaining silent."

"If the child is not held, hugged, cuddled, or loved, its development will be impaired and its brain will not mature properly."

"Happiness doesn't always come from a pursuit. Sometimes it comes when we least expect it."

"It is under the greatest adversity that there exists the greatest potential for doing good, both for oneself and others."

"We need to learn to want what we have, not to have what we want, in order to get stable and steady happiness."

"When you talk, you are only repeating what you already know. But if you listen, you may learn something new."

"Open-minded people tend to be interested in Buddhism because Buddha urged people to investigate things – he didn't just command them to believe."

"Climate change is not the concern of just one or two nations. It is an issue that affects the whole of humanity and every living being on this earth."

"Because of lack of moral principle, human life becomes worthless. Moral principle, truthfulness, is a key factor. If we lose that, then there is no future."

"When the heart is closed it leads to fear, stress and anger. Nurturing the idea of the oneness of humanity has the effect of opening the heart."

"The whole purpose of religion is to facilitate love and compassion, patience, tolerance, humility, and forgiveness."

"Only the development of compassion and understanding for others can bring us the tranquility and happiness we all seek."

"The creatures that inhabit this earth-be they human beings or animals-are here to contribute, each in its own particular way, to the beauty and prosperity of the world."

"A good friend who points out mistakes and imperfections and rebukes evil is to be respected as if he reveals the secret of some hidden treasure."

"Anger or hatred is like a fisherman's hook. It is very important for us to ensure that we are not caught by it."

"If someone has a gun and is trying to kill you, it would be reasonable to shoot back with your own gun."

"We need to learn how to want what we have NOT to have what we want in order to get steady and stable Happiness"

"Our ancient experience confirms at every point that everything is linked together, everything is inseparable."

"Although you may not always be able to avoid difficult situations, you can modify the extent to which you can suffer by how you choose to respond to the situation."

"Hard times build determination and inner strength. Through them we can also come to appreciate the uselessness of anger. Instead of getting angry nurture a deep caring and respect for troublemakers because by creating such trying circumstances they provide us with invaluable opportunities to practice tolerance and patience."

"The topic of compassion is not at all religious business; it is important to know it is human business, it is a question of human survival."

"A truly compassionate attitude toward others does not change even if they behave negatively or hurt you."

"Compassion is not religious business, it is human business, it is not luxury, it is essential for our own peace and mental stability, it is essential for human survival."

"Time passes unhindered. When we make mistakes, we cannot turn the clock back and try again. All we can do is use the present well."

"All suffering is caused by ignorance. People inflict pain on others in the selfish pursuit of their own happiness or satisfaction"

"In our struggle for freedom, truth is the only weapon we possess." "Let us try to recognize the precious nature of each day."

"Give the ones you love wings to fly, roots to come back and reasons to stay." "We can never obtain peace in the outer world until we make peace with ourselves"

"The planet does not need more successful people. The planet desperately needs more peacemakers, healers, restorers, storytellers, and lovers of all kinds."

"Real change in the world will only come from a change of heart." "Know the rules well, so you can break them effectively."

"When we meet real tragedy in life, we can react in two ways–either by losing hope and falling into self-destructive habits, or by using the challenge to find our inner strength."

"I defeat my enemies when I make them my friends." "Someone else's action should not determine your response."

"Inner peace is the key: if you have inner peace, the external problems do not affect your deep sense of peace and tranquility...without this inner peace, no matter how comfortable your life is materially, you may still be worried, disturbed, or unhappy because of circumstances."

"Silence is sometimes the best answer" "It is necessary to help others not in our prayers but in our daily lives."

"Where ignorance is our master, there is no possibility of real peace."
"Remember that sometimes not getting what you want is a wonderful stroke of luck."

"I believe the very purpose of our life is to seek happiness. Whether one believes in religion or not, whether one believes in that religion or this religion, we are all seeking something better in life. So, I think, the very motion of our life is towards happiness.

"Irrespective of whether we are believers or agnostics, whether we believe in God or karma, moral ethics is a code which everyone is able to pursue."

"The ultimate source of happiness is not money and power, but warm-heartedness" "Many of our problems stem from attitudes like putting ourselves first at all costs."

"The more you are motivated by love, the more fearless and free your action will be." "Just one small positive thought in the morning can change your whole day."

"It is very rare or almost impossible that an event can be negative from all points of view." "It is necessary to help others not in our prayers but in our daily lives."

"Choose to be optimistic, it feels better." "Dissatisfaction is the seed of anger." "Neither a space station nor an enlightened mind can be realized in a day."

"No matter how educated or wealthy you are, if you don't have peace of mind, you won't be happy." ~ Dalai Lama

"People take different roads seeking fulfillment and happiness. Just because they're not on your road does not mean they are lost."

"The roots of all goodness lie in the soil of appreciation for goodness."
"Judge your success by what you had to give up in order to get it."

"People must first accomplish internal disarmament before aiming aiming for external disarmament" "In the practice of tolerance, one's enemy is the best teacher."

"Be happy to change your goals, but never change your values" "Do not let the behavior of others destroy your inner peace.""Through violence, you may 'solve' one problem, but you sow the seeds for another."

"To conquer oneself is a greater victory than to conquer thousands in a battle." "Do not let the behavior of others destroy your inner peace."

"If you don't love yourself, you cannot love others." "When you lose, don't lose the lesson.""There are always problems to face, but it makes a difference if our minds are calm.""Sleep is the best meditation.""Look at situations from all angles, and you will become more open.""When you practice gratefulness, there is a sense of respect toward others.""When we feel love and kindness toward others, it not only makes others feel loved and cared for, but it helps us also to develop inner happiness and peace.""If you think you are too small to make a difference, try sleeping with a mosquito."

"I find hope in the darkest days, and focus in the brightest.
"The goal is not to be better than the other man, but your previous self."
"Remember that the best relationship is one in which your love for each other exceeds your need for each other.
"A spoon cannot taste of the food it carries. Likewise, a foolish man cannot understand the wise man´s wisdom even if he associates with a sage."

CPSIA information can be obtained
at www.ICGtesting.com
Printed in the USA
BVHW042356220623
666253BV00006B/670